A Day in the Life: Rain Forest Animals

Lemur

Anita Ganeri

Heinemann Library
Chicago, IL

www.heinemannraintree.com

Visit our website to find out more information about Heinemann-Raintree books.

To order:

☎ Phone 888-454-2279

🖥 Visit www.heinemannraintree.com to browse our catalog and order online.

©2011 Heinemann Library
an imprint of Capstone Global Library, LLC
Chicago, Illinois

Edited by Nancy Dickmann, Rebecca Rissman, and Catherine Veitch
Designed by Steve Mead
Picture research by Mica Brancic
Originated by Capstone Global Library
Printed and bound in China by South China Printing Company Ltd

14 13 12 11 10
10 9 8 7 6 5 4 3 2 1

Library of Congress Cataloging-in-Publication Data
Ganeri, Anita, 1961-
   Lemur / Anita Ganeri.—1st ed.
      p. cm.—(A day in the life. Rain forest animals)
   Includes bibliographical references and index.
   ISBN 978-1-4329-4111-6 (hc)—ISBN 978-1-4329-4122-2 (pb) 1. Lemur (Genus)—Juvenile literature. I. Title.
   QL737.P95G36 2011
   599.8'3—dc22   2010001134

Acknowledgments
We would like to thank the following for permission to reproduce photographs: Alamy pp. 10 (© Martin Harvey), 20 (© Fotosonline/Peter Kelly); Ardea pp. 6 (M. Watson), 16 (Thomas Marent); Corbis p. 12 (Encyclopedia/© Gallo Images); FLPA pp. 4, 19, 23 mammal (David Hosking), 15, 23 fossa (Ariadne Van Zandbergen), 17 (Jurgen & Christine Sohns), 21 (Albert Visage), 22 (Minden Pictures/Thomas Marent); Photolibrary pp. 5 (John Warburton-Lee Photography/Nigel Pavitt), 7, 9, 13, 23 tuft (Tips Italia/John Devries), 11 (Picture Press/ Jurgen & Christine Sohns), 18 (Oxford Scientific (OSF)/David Haring/DUPC); Photoshot pp. 14, 23 troop (NHPA/Kevin Schafer); Shutterstock p. 23 rain forest (© Szefei).

Cover photograph of a black and white ruffed lemur hanging upside down in a tree reproduced with permission of Getty Images (Gallo Images/Martin Harvey).

Back cover photographs of (left) fossa reproduced with permission of FLPA (Ariadne Van Zandbergen); and (right) young lemur reproduced with permission of FLPA (David Hosking).

We would like to thank Michael Bright for his invaluable help in the preparation of this book.

Every effort has been made to contact copyright holders of material reproduced in this book. Any omissions will be rectified in subsequent printings if notice is given to the publisher.

Contents

What Is a Lemur? 4

What Do Lemurs Look Like? 6

Where Do Lemurs Live? 8

What Do Lemurs Do During the Day? 10

What Do Lemurs Eat? 12

Do Lemurs Live in Groups? 14

What Do Lemurs Sound Like? 16

Where Are Baby Lemurs Born? 18

What Do Lemurs Do at Night? 20

Lemur Body Map 22

Glossary 23

Find Out More 24

Index 24

Some words are in bold, **like this**. You can find them in the glossary on page 23.

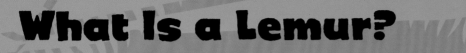

What Is a Lemur?

A lemur is a **mammal**.

Many mammals have hairy bodies and feed their babies milk.

indri

There are many different types of lemurs.

The biggest lemur is the indri.

tail

Lemurs have long arms and legs and often have long tails.

Their strong hands and fingers help them to climb trees.

Lemurs have thick fur that can be brown, black, white, or red.

This lemur has **tufts** of fur around its neck.

Where Do Lemurs Live?

Madagascar

Lemurs live on the island of Madagascar in the Indian Ocean.

Wild lemurs are not found anywhere else on Earth.

The lemurs in this book live in the **rain forests** in Madagascar.

In a rain forest, it is warm and wet all year long.

What Do Lemurs Do During the Day?

Many types of lemurs wake up when the sun rises.

They spend the morning moving through the trees looking for food.

In the afternoon, some lemurs like to rest in the sun.

They sit on a branch and stretch their arms out wide.

Lemurs eat fruit, leaves, and seeds.

A lemur also uses its long tongue to reach deep inside flowers for food.

Some lemurs hang upside down from trees to feed.

They hang onto the branches with their feet.

Do Lemurs Live in Groups?

Many lemurs live in groups of up to 20 animals.

A group is called a **troop**.

fossa

Living in a group helps to keep the lemurs safe.

It is easier for an animal such as a **fossa** to attack one lemur rather than a group.

What Do Lemurs Sound Like?

Lemurs make a lot of different sounds.

They wail, scream, snort, yap, and groan.

These sounds help the lemurs to keep in touch with one another.

They also warn other groups of lemurs to stay in their own space.

Where Are Baby Lemurs Born?

Some baby lemurs are born in nests in the treetops.

A female lemur builds the nest out of twigs, leaves, and moss.

baby

During the day, female lemurs carry their babies with them as they look for food.

Baby lemurs cling to their mother's belly or back.

What Do Lemurs Do at Night?

In the evening, lemurs look for more food to eat.

Then they go to sleep on a branch or in a hollow tree.

Some rain forest lemurs look for food at night.

Other lemurs move around from time to time during the day and night.

Lemur Body Map

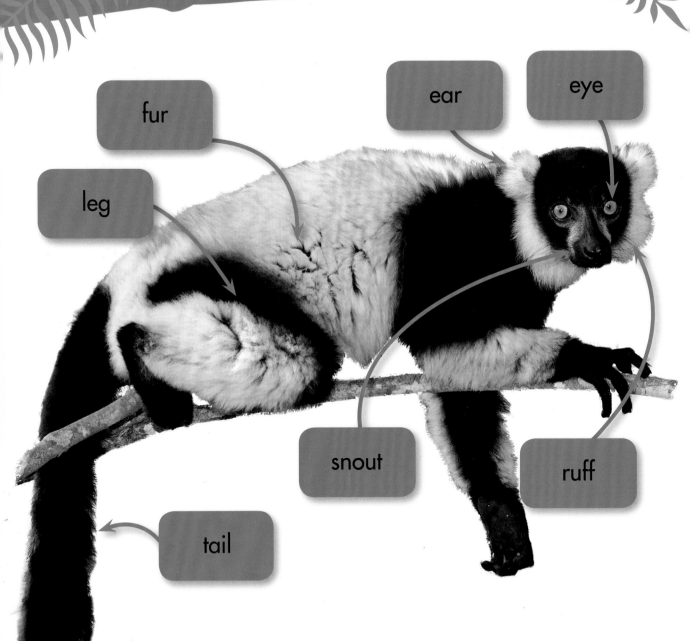

fur

leg

ear

eye

snout

ruff

tail

Glossary

 **fossa** meat-eating animal that lives in Madagascar

 **mammal** animal that feeds its babies milk. Most mammals have hair or fur.

 **rain forest** thick forest with very tall trees and a lot of rain

 **troop** group of lemurs

 **tuft** bunch of something, such as fur, that grows from the same place

Lemur

Can you find these in the book?

fossa

baby

When you want to find out...

Heinemann **Read and Learn**

About the author: Anita Ganeri is an award-winning author of nonfiction books for young people. She has written many books about animals and the natural world.

Book consultant: Michael Bright has traveled all over the world to film animals in action for the BBC Natural History Unit. He has also written books about sharks and other animals.

Anaconda	978 1 4329 4123 9
Capybara	978 1 4329 4121 5
Howler Monkey	978 1 4329 4124 6
Jaguar	978 1 4329 4117 8
Lemur	978 1 4329 4122 2
Macaw	978 1 4329 4116 1
Orangutan	978 1 4329 4118 5
Piranha	978 1 4329 4119 2
Poison Dart Frog	978 1 4329 4115 4
Tarantula	978 1 4329 4120 8

The **A Day in the Life: Rain Forest Animals** series looks at a typical day and night in the lives of different types of rain forest animals. There is also a body map in each title that labels parts of the animal's body.

Read and Learn is an extensive collection of nonfiction books that help young readers discover and understand the world around them. Headings in the form of questions help children to focus and ask their own questions. **Read and Learn** books contain intriguing pictures, a glossary, and an index, offering young readers an introduction to these important features of nonfiction text.

Primary Life Sciences

Heinemann Raintree

heinemannraintree.com

ISBN 978-1-4329-4122-2

9 781432 941222

Level K